MOVING FORWARD

written by

Chris Barton

illustrated by

Steffi Walthall

**FROM SPACE-AGE RIDES
TO CIVIL RIGHTS SIT-INS
WITH AIRMAN ALTON YATES**

BEACH LANE BOOKS

New York London Toronto Sydney New Delhi

When Alton Yates was growing up, he had a neighbor living right next door who had gone to war in 1918.

Alton would listen to Mr. Jeffcoat's stories—stories about dangers he faced in World War I and stories about coming home afterward.

Mr. Jeffcoat had thought that when he got back, things would be different there in Jacksonville.

when their service was complete?
Wouldn't they at least be able to vote?

Not in Florida. Not in the South. Not under Jim Crow, the name for the system of laws keeping Black people—even veterans— apart from and underneath the whites.

Alton saw sailors and soldiers return from World War II and experience the same disappointment.

Then he saw it happen all over again to those who had fought in Korea.

And yet, Alton could hardly wait to join the Air Force.

Part of it was inspiration.

Air Force Captain Daniel "Chappie" James had come to Alton's junior high school and declared to students,

"I am an American warrior."

Alton could imagine that for himself.

Part of it was hopefulness.

Hadn't President Truman ordered the end of racial segregation—of keeping different groups separate and treating them unequally—in the military? Wasn't the Air Force the first of the armed services to actually make that change? Wouldn't that make for a better life than what Jacksonville had to offer?

And part of it was reality.

Alton's mother died when her seventh child was still a toddler. Now Alton had to think of his dad, his grandmother, and his younger siblings. He needed more education, but his family couldn't afford college.

Alton enlisted in the Air Force in 1955. He knew that serving his country, whatever it required, was his way forward.

But how far forward? Alton had no idea until the day he met Lieutenant Colonel John Paul Stapp—the Fastest Human on Earth.

At Holloman Air Force Base out in the New Mexico desert, Stapp had ridden a rocket-powered sled called *Sonic Wind* as it roared from zero to 639 miles per hour in only five seconds.

The sled and Stapp then came to a stop—in less than a second and a half.

That ride was physically punishing. Stapp came away with two black eyes. He had bruises and blisters. But along with his injuries, he also had a mission that made his wounds worthwhile.

Stapp was dedicated to researching what dangers human bodies could survive in airplanes, spacecraft, and even automobiles—if they had proper protection. And he needed help figuring out how best to protect them.

Pilots were flying faster and higher than ever before—faster than the speed of sound, and approaching 100,000 feet above the ground. This was the future. There was so much progress for Stapp to keep up with, so many changes to make. For that, he needed a good team.

Alton stepped up, volunteered for the job, and accepted the hazards it entailed.

He soon found himself strapped into the Bopper sled . . .
pulled back tightly like a slingshot . . .

then surging ahead with tremendous force . . .

and brought to a sudden stop.

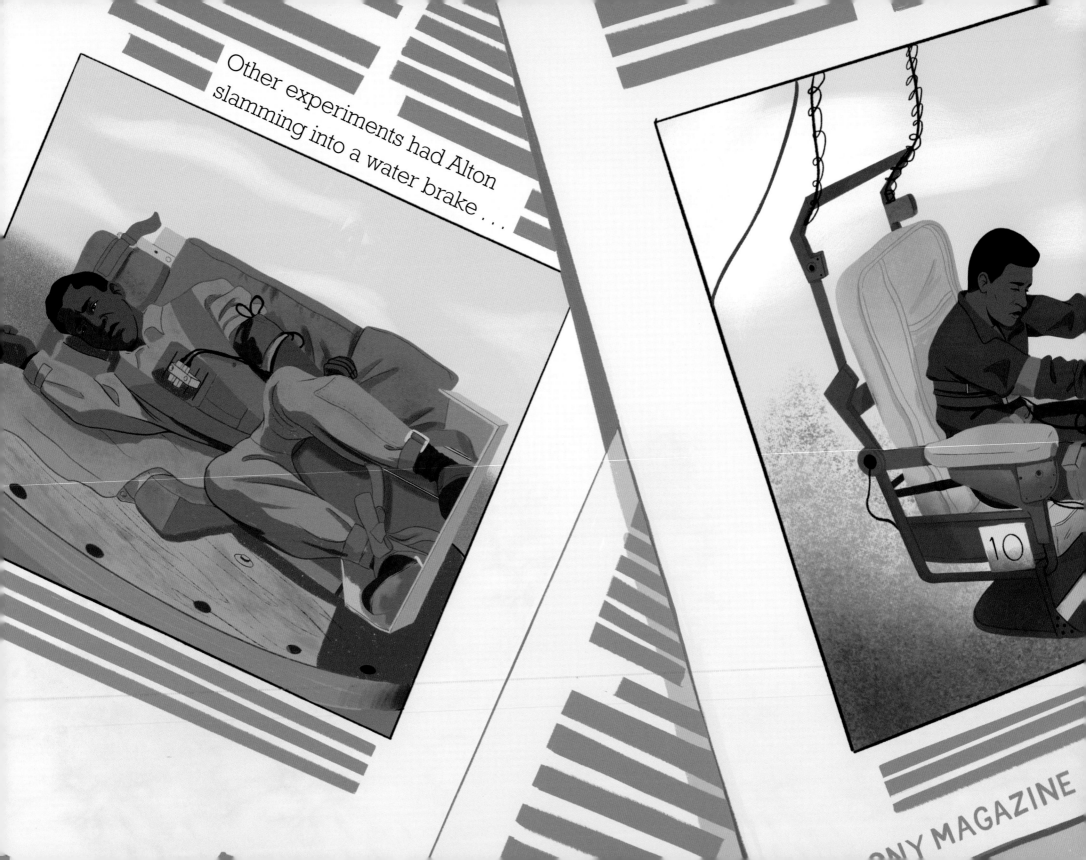

Other experiments had Alton slamming into a water brake . . .

submerging . . .

and so forth.

EBONY MAGAZINE

Alton experienced sharp pains during some of those tests. His aches could last for weeks. But warriors should not expect to always walk away unscathed.

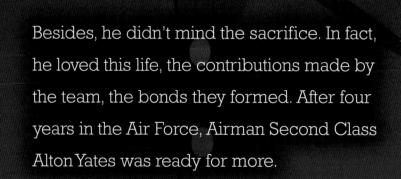

Besides, he didn't mind the sacrifice. In fact, he loved this life, the contributions made by the team, the bonds they formed. After four years in the Air Force, Airman Second Class Alton Yates was ready for more.

One day, though, his grandmother called from Jacksonville. Alton's dad was very sick, and she needed help with Alton's younger sister and brother. The Air Force granted Alton an honorable discharge.

So in the fall of 1959, Alton dressed up in his Air Force blues, got into his Pontiac Chieftain, and headed for home.

NO COLORED
ALLOWED

Maybe ninety minutes later, Alton
crossed the state line into Texas.

Back into the South.

Back under Jim Crow.

Alton stopped for a cup of coffee, and got kicked out of the restaurant.

He stopped to gas up his car, and got kicked out of the service station when he asked to use the restroom.

With curses and slurs, the man in charge wouldn't even let him buy a sandwich.

TEXAS
STATE LINE

Alton found a grocery store where he could buy bread, peanut butter, and jelly. That's nearly all he ate as he drove the next 1,700 miles across the same United States for which he'd risked his body dozens of times. To use the bathroom, he had to go into the woods.

Through Texas, and Louisiana, and Mississippi, and Alabama, and Georgia, and finally across Florida, Alton was angry.

All alone, he had many hours to think about just how angry he was. To think about the equality, respect, and basic dignity he had experienced in his four years at Holloman. To think about how all that now lay miles behind him.

Acting out of frustration and putting himself in extra peril on the route home wouldn't do a thing to help anyone. But by the time Alton made it to Jacksonville, he had a new mission.

Before, he had met the challenge of physical forces. Now he would square off against a social one.

He would make a stand against Jim Crow.

This was his future now.

Ending segregation in this place that seemed stuck in the past was every bit as urgent as Alton's work in the Air Force.

And in Jacksonville, being part of a good team was every bit as important as it had been while striving for progress at Holloman.

After his dad died, Alton got active in an organization called the NAACP Youth Council, working alongside other young adults and teenagers. At twenty-three, he was the vice president and one of the oldest members. The president, Rodney Hurst, was sixteen, and so was fellow officer Marjorie Meeks.

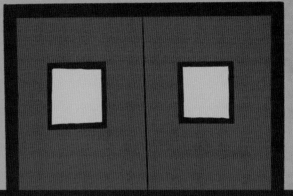

Other members included kids as young as thirteen, but they were kids committed to a cause: combating racism and fighting for their civil rights as Americans.

One battlefront was downtown
Jacksonville. Woolworth's,
W. T. Grant's, and other department
stores would let Black customers
spend their money shopping
there. Yet the lunch counters in
those same stores were for
white diners only.

Sharing a meal together allows people to get to know one another and experience what they have in common. But Jim Crow kept those who weren't white from being seen, and known, and treated as people.

In August 1960, the Youth Council strove to put an end to that by staging Saturday sit-ins.

After meeting up at the Laura Street Presbyterian Church, Alton and other protesters walked to the stores and peacefully parked themselves at the lunch counters.

The store managers shut down the lunch counters for the day rather than serve Black and white customers side by side. Many white people got upset, and some of them got vicious.

They hurled hateful, nasty words at the protesters. They threatened them. They jabbed them with pins and sharp sticks.

Members of the Youth Council were ready for all of that. And they were ready to remain nonviolent in the face of it—even those who had once aspired to be American warriors.

How, though, could they possibly have been ready for what they faced on August 27?

Scores—some say hundreds—of white men gathered at nearby Hemming Park that morning. They handed out hard wooden ax handles.

Several brought baseball bats.

Some even carried flags or wore uniforms of the Confederate army—an army that ninety-nine years earlier had gone to war against the United States.

The danger was obvious. Organizers for the Youth Council saw what they were up against. The members—most of them children, remember—voted to protest anyway.

Alton had gotten married only eight days earlier. His new bride, Gwen, waited at home with Alton's younger sister and brother. They had no idea of the confrontation that was unfolding downtown.

When Alton and other protesters arrived at Woolworth's to take their places at the lunch counter, the white men began to attack.

The mob seemed to swing their ax handles and baseball bats at any brown body they came to, no matter how young, no matter how outnumbered.

The protesters scattered. The police looked the other way.

At that moment, Holloman Air Force Base was far away.
But Alton's commitment to his country was not. His
willingness to put his safety on the line—to put his
very life on the line—could not have been closer.

In the chaos, a white man swung his
club through the humid morning air . . .

and struck Alton Yates on the back of his head.

Fifty-seven years later, at the dinner table with
Gwen in their Jacksonville home, Alton Yates
touches the scar from that blow.

Since Alton acquired that scar, spaceflight took properly protected Americans to the moon and back. John Paul Stapp's research—including the pains and aches endured by Alton and others—made car travel much safer. Chappie James, who so inspired Alton, became the first African American four-star general.

It was not fast or easy, but Jacksonville institutions have progressed from pretending Ax Handle Saturday never happened to honoring the NAACP Youth Council's fight for civil rights.

That's some word, "fight." Same with "warrior."

Being a warrior doesn't mean being violent.
And a person's willingness to be violent doesn't
make their cause noble or right or worthwhile.

But a willingness to fight for
what's just and what's fair—that
willingness is what has made
the United States of Alton
Yates's life a work in progress.

Sometimes, that progress is hard to see.

Sometimes, things may seem to be moving backward.

But Alton remains optimistic. From where he peacefully stands, that forward motion continues.

TIME LINE

1861–65: In an effort to preserve slavery, the Confederacy—including the state of Florida—starts, fights, and loses the Civil War.

1885: Florida's new state constitution includes Jim Crow provisions discriminating against Black people.

1898: A towering Confederate monument is installed in a downtown Jacksonville park. The park is later renamed for Charles Hemming, the Confederate veteran who donated the monument.

1900: "Lift Every Voice and Sing," written by Jacksonville native James Weldon Johnson and his brother and eventually known as the Black National Anthem, is performed for the first time.

1907: The US Army establishes an aeronautical division, which later becomes the US Air Force.

1917–18: Black members of the US armed forces serve in World War I.

1936: Alton Yates is born in Jacksonville, Florida. The National Association for the Advancement of Colored People (NAACP) establishes its Youth and College Division.

1941–45: Black members of the US armed forces serve in World War II.

1947: Air Force Captain Chuck Yeager, flying a Bell X-1, becomes the first person to break the sound barrier.

1948: President Harry S. Truman signs Executive Order 9981, which begins the process of desegregating the US armed forces. The Air Force moves the most quickly to achieve this.

1950–53: Black members of US armed forces serve in the Korean War.

1951: Air Force Captain Daniel "Chappie" James visits Alton's junior high.

1953: Alton's mother dies. Holloman Air Force Base in New Mexico becomes the home of the Aeromedical Field Laboratory (AFL), which had been created two years earlier to conduct experiments on animal, dummy, and—eventually—human test subjects.

1954: At Holloman, Lieutenant Colonel (and physician) John Paul Stapp travels 639 miles per hour in a rocket-powered sled called *Sonic Wind*.

1955: Alton graduates from high school, enlists in the Air Force, and is assigned to Holloman. In Jacksonville, junior high student Rodney Hurst begins attending meetings of the NAACP Youth Council, which is advised by history teacher Rutledge Pearson. (Rodney's classmate Marjorie Meeks joins the following year.)

1955–59: Alton voluntarily participates in AFL experiments known as the Bopper, the Daisy Track, and the Swing Seat, as well as centrifuge tests, underwater gravity tests, and car crash studies; he receives hazard pay. The US government creates the National Aeronautics and Space Administration (NASA).

1959: Alton is featured in the May issue of *Ebony* magazine ("GI risks death 65 times for science") and in October leaves the Air Force to return to Jacksonville. A new high school in Jacksonville is named for Nathan Bedford Forrest, a Confederate general and early leader of the Ku Klux Klan terrorist group.

1960: Alton's father dies. In February, four Black students sit in at a Woolworth's in Greensboro, North Carolina, beginning a wave of demonstrations to integrate lunch counters throughout the South. Alton becomes active in the Jacksonville NAACP Youth Council, which conducts sit-ins at lunch counters near Hemming Park on August 13 and 20. The protesters are attacked by a mob of white men on August 27, which becomes known as Ax Handle Saturday. After being struck in the head in Woolworth's, Alton escapes through a side door to safety in a nearby church. The major newspaper in Jacksonville, the *Florida Times-Union*, fails to cover the protests or the attacks.

1961: Jacksonville lunch counters are integrated.

1969–72: Supported by research performed on Holloman's Daisy Track, NASA astronauts travel to the moon and back.

1975: Chappie James becomes the first African American four-star general.

1984: Building on John Paul Stapp's research, US states begin requiring the use of seat belts in cars, saving thousands of lives each year.

2002: A small historical marker commemorating the 1960 sit-ins and Ax Handle Saturday is installed in the renamed Hemming Plaza.

2020: The Confederate monument is removed from Hemming Plaza, which is renamed James Weldon Johnson Park. The *Florida Times-Union* apologizes for its journalistic failures sixty years earlier. Alton and Gwen Yates celebrate their sixtieth wedding anniversary.

AUTHOR'S NOTE

I first learned about Alton Yates in fall 2016 when I heard him and his daughter, journalist Toni Yates, on the StoryCorps podcast discussing his experimental Air Force service at the dawn of the Space Age.

When I read about Alton's activism that soon followed—and about the racist assault that Jacksonville's brave young civil rights protesters encountered on Ax Handle Saturday—I was startled by the fact that great advances in science and technology could take place at the same time as such a primitive expression of hateful, ignorant cultural attitudes.

I shouldn't have been surprised. In the United States, events of recent years have made clear that both of these opposing forces continue.

But despite many obstacles, so does social progress. So does commitment toward more widespread justice and equality. And so does the endlessly renewable courage of people young and old to carry on the work of transforming this country into a more perfect union. It is our most worthwhile mission.

Alton Yates in 2021, in response to Chris Barton's question, "What do you hope that people will take from the story of your experiences at Holloman and in 1960?":

"I hope that they will come away with a greater sense of optimism about the future of our country. It's old-fashioned, in a sense, to talk about how much you love America, and what America has been, and what America has done, the goodness of its people, the sacrifices that have been made for us to reach the point where we are. None of that could have happened without a good deal of support of some people whose voices you don't hear ordinarily. I mean, there are people who kind of remain silent, in the background, but they assist where they can. I would hope that people would see the goodness of the American people, and that the spirit of America still lives, that we are still, in my opinion, the greatest nation on the face of this earth. We have our flaws. We have things that sometimes we're not very proud of. But overall, we're still a people who realizes, I think, and appreciates the fact that we have been truly blessed. And that we have an obligation to share those blessings, or the fruit of those blessings, with others. And that we do so at any and every opportunity we are given. I just want people to see the goodness of America."

ILLUSTRATOR'S NOTE

Learning about Alton Yates and Ax Handle Saturday has been such an emotional and humbling experience. However, Alton's story is an example of persisting despite how unjust and cruel the world and society can be and continuing moving forward to create a better world for those that follow. My hope is that this book brings Alton, and his contemporaries whose lives were so impactful to all of us, the recognition they deserve. And I hope that we take their stories and honor them with our lives and our actions.

SELECTED SOURCES

The author's research for this book included trips to both Jacksonville and Holloman Air Force Base and many conversations with Alton Yates via phone, email, text, and Zoom, as well as over a homemade spaghetti dinner.

Bartley, Abel A. *Keeping the Faith: Race, Politics, and Social Development in Jacksonville, Florida, 1940-1970*. Westport, CT: Greenwood Press, 2000.

Brown, Marjorie Meeks. Telephone interview by author, April 23, 2020.

Hurst, Rodney L. Sr. *It Was Never about a Hot Dog and a Coke! A Personal Account of the 1960 Sit-in Demonstrations in Jacksonville, Florida, and Ax Handle Saturday*. Livermore, California: WingSpan Press, 2008.

McGovern, James R. *Black Eagle: General Daniel "Chappie" James Jr.* Tuscaloosa: University of Alabama Press, 1985.

Meeter, George F. *The Holloman Story: Eyewitness Accounts of Space Age Research*. Albuquerque: University of New Mexico Press, 1967.

Murphy, Bridget. "Ax Handle Saturday: Alton Yates Risked His Life for a Principle," *Florida Times-Union*, August 27, 2010.

Ryan, Craig. *Sonic Wind: The Story of John Paul Stapp and How a Renegade Doctor Became the Fastest Man on Earth*. New York: Liveright, 2015.

Yates, Alton. Interview by Kristin Dodek, February 16, 2005. Samuel Proctor Oral History Program Collection, P.K. Yonge Library of Florida History, University of Florida.

Yates, Alton. "My Incredible Journey," *Friends Journal* 37, no. 4 (Winter 2014–2015): 9–13.

A complete bibliography for this book is available at chrisbarton.info/book /movingforward.

To Alton and Gwen Yates, to all who inspired
them, and to all whom they inspire

—C. B.

Gwen and Alton Yates at their home in Jacksonville, with
author Chris Barton on July 13, 2017. Photo by Jennifer Ziegler.

To my family and friends—this book
wouldn't exist like this without you

—S. W.

BEACH LANE BOOKS

An imprint of Simon & Schuster Children's Publishing Division

1230 Avenue of the Americas, New York, New York 10020

Text © 2022 by Chris Barton

Illustration © 2022 by Steffi Walthall

Book design by Greg Stadnyk © 2022 by Simon & Schuster, Inc.

For information about special discounts for bulk purchases, please contact Simon & Schuster Special Sales at 1-866-506-1949
or business@simonandschuster.com.

The Simon & Schuster Speakers Bureau can bring authors to your live event. For more information or to book an event, contact the Simon & Schuster Speakers Bureau at
1-866-248-3049 or visit our website at www.simonspeakers.com.

The text for this book was set in Rockwell.

The illustrations for this book were rendered digitally.

Manufactured in China

1021 SCP

First Edition

2 4 6 8 10 9 7 5 3 1

Library of Congress Cataloging-in-Publication Data

Names: Barton, Chris, author. | Walthall, Steffi, illustrator.

Title: Moving forward: from space-age rides to Civil Rights sit-ins with Airman Alton Yates / Chris Barton ; illustrated by Steffi Walthall.

Other titles: From space-age rides to Civil Rights sit-ins with Airman Alton Yates

Description: First edition. | New York, New York : Beach Lane Books, [2022] | Includes bibliographical references. | Audience: Ages 4-8 | Audience: Grades 2-3 | Summary: "A
picture book biography on Alton Yates, a Black man who served in the Air Force in the 1950s and contributed to key research on flight safety for pilots and passengers. After
returning home, Alton dedicated his life to standing against Jim Crow and fighting for racial equality"— Provided by publisher.

Identifiers: LCCN 2021003793 (print) | LCCN 2021003794 (ebook) | ISBN 9781534473652 (hardcover) | ISBN 9781534473669 (ebook)

Subjects: LCSH: Yates, Alton, 1936—Juvenile literature. | Airmen—United States—Biography—Juvenile literature. | African Americans—Florida—Jacksonville—Biography—Juvenile
literature. | African Americans—Civil rights—Florida—Jacksonville—History—Juvenile literature. | African American civil rights workers—Florida—Jacksonville—Biography—
Juvenile literature. | Civil rights workers—Florida—Jacksonville—Biography—Juvenile literature. | Jacksonville (Fla.)—Biography—Juvenile literature. | Jacksonville (Fla.)—Race
relations—Juvenile literature.

Classification: LCC F319.J1 B378 2022 (print) | LCC F319.J1 (ebook) | DDC 323.092 [B]—dc23

LC record available at https://lccn.loc.gov/2021003793

LC ebook record available at https://lccn.loc.gov/2021003794